12/16

P9-DZP-210

The
United States Presidents

DONALD TRUMP

Jill C. Wheeler

Checkerboard Library

An Imprint of Abdo Publishing
abdopublishing.com

abdopublishing.com

Published by Abdo Publishing, a division of ABDO, PO Box 398166, Minneapolis, MN 55439.
Copyright © 2017 by Abdo Consulting Group, Inc. International copyrights reserved in all countries.
No part of this book may be reproduced in any form without written permission from the publisher.
Checkerboard Library™ is a trademark and logo of Abdo Publishing.

Printed in the United States of America, North Mankato, Minnesota.
112016
012017

THIS BOOK CONTAINS
RECYCLED MATERIALS

Cover Photo: Dreamstime
Interior Photos: Alamy pp. 9, 13, 15, 21, 23, 27, 29; AP Images pp. 5, 18, 20, 25; Dreamstime pp.
    17, 19; Wikimedia Commons p. 11

Editors: Tamara L. Britton, Bridget O'Brien
Art Direction & Cover Design: Neil Klinepier

Publisher's Cataloging-in-Publication Data

Names: Wheeler, Jill C., author.
Title: Donald Trump / by Jill C. Wheeler.
Description: Minneapolis, MN : Abdo Publishing, 2017. | Series: The United States
    presidents | Includes bibliographical references and index.
Identifiers: LCCN 2016954381 | ISBN 9781680783636 (lib. bdg.) |
    ISBN 9781680795141 (ebook)
Subjects: LCSH: Trump, Donald, 1946- --Juvenile literature. | Presidential
    candidates--United States-- Biography--Juvenile literature. | Political
    campaigns--United States--Biography--Juvenile literature. | Presidents--
    United States--Biography--Election, 2016--Juvenile literature.
Classification: DDC 973.932/092 [B]--dc23
LC record available at http://lccn.loc.gov/2016954381

Contents

DONALD TRUMP

On November 8, 2016, Donald Trump was elected the forty-fifth president of the United States. He was the first president in more than 60 years who had never served as a governor or a congressman.

Trump was a successful **real estate** developer. He had made millions of dollars with his smart **negotiating** skills. As president, he thought he could use these skills to improve the country's **economic** and foreign policies. His campaign slogan was "Make America Great Again."

The 2016 election was historic in other ways. Trump's opponent was **Democrat** Hillary Clinton. Clinton was the first major-party female candidate for president. She had served as a US senator and **secretary of state**. She had been First Lady when her husband William J. "Bill" Clinton served as the forty-second president.

Trump faced a strong opponent. But when Americans went to the polls on Election Day, they chose Trump. They responded to his message of strengthening the economy, controlling **immigration**, and reforming the Affordable Care Act.

TIMELINE

1946 - On June 14, Donald John Trump was born in Queens, New York.

1964 - Trump graduated from the New York Military Academy.

1968 - Trump graduated from the University of Pennsylvania.

1971 - Trump took over his family's business. He renamed it the Trump Organization.

1977 - On April 7, Trump and Ivana Zelníčková were married.

1980 - The Grand Hyatt New York, Trump's first major development project, opened in New York City, New York.

1983 - Trump Tower opened.

1987 - *The Art of the Deal* was published.

1993 - On December 20, Trump and Marla Maples were married.

1997 - *The Art of the Comeback* was published.

2004 - *The Apprentice* began.

2005 - Trump and Melania Knauss were married on January 22.

2008 - *The Celebrity Apprentice* began.

2015 - On June 16, Trump announced his candidacy for president.

2016 - Trump became the Republican Party's nominee on July 19.

2017 - On January 20, Trump took office as the forty-fifth US president.

DID YOU KNOW?

Trump's birthday, June 14, is Flag Day.

Trump has written sixteen books, all of them best sellers.

First Lady Melania Trump speaks five languages.

Trump's sister Maryanne Trump Barry is an appeals court judge. She was nominated to that post by former president Bill Clinton.

Melania Trump is only the second First Lady born outside of the United States. Louisa Adams, wife of the sixth US president John Quincy Adams, was the first.

FAMILY BUSINESS

Donald John Trump was born on June 14, 1946, in the New York City, New York **borough** of Queens. His parents were Frederick C. Trump and Mary Trump. Donald's father was in the construction and **real estate** business. His mother was a homemaker. Donald had four **siblings**. They were Maryanne, Elizabeth, Robert, and Fred Jr.

Fred Trump's parents were German **immigrants**. Mary Trump immigrated to the United States from Scotland in 1929. She met Fred at a dance. They married in 1936. The Trump family business was successful. The family became wealthy. Yet Fred and Mary worked to teach their children the value of money. They learned this through hard work and **thrift**. Donald was reminded to turn out all the lights in the house. At mealtimes, his parents expected him to eat every bit of food on his plate.

FAST FACTS

BORN - June 14, 1946
WIVES - Ivana Zelníčková (1949–)
Marla Maples (1963–)
Melania Knauss (1970–)
CHILDREN - 5
POLITICAL PARTY - Republican
AGE AT INAUGURATION - 70
YEARS SERVED - 2017–
VICE PRESIDENT - Mike Pence

Donald's father also insisted his children have summer jobs. Donald and his **siblings** often went to work with Fred. They picked up cans at the building sites to return for the five-cent deposit. Donald also had a paper route.

Trump with his parents

SCHOOL DAYS

Donald attended Kew-Forest School nearby Forest Hills, New York. But his parents thought Donald needed more **discipline**. So in 1959 when Donald was 13, his parents sent him to the New York Military Academy (NYMA).

Donald did well at NYMA. He was one of the highest-ranking members of his class. He played on the varsity soccer, baseball, and football teams.

Donald graduated from NYMA in 1964. He then entered Fordham University in New York City. Two years later, he transferred to the University of Pennsylvania. There, Donald studied **economics** at the Wharton School.

On weekends, Donald often went home to New York City. There, he worked with his father to learn the **real estate** business. One summer his father purchased a run-down apartment complex in Ohio. Donald **renovated** the building and later sold it for a profit.

Trump was captain of the baseball team at NYMA.

GRAND PLANS

Trump graduated from college in 1968. Then he went to work for his father's company. Fred Trump had made a fortune building middle-class housing in New York City's outer **boroughs**. One of Trump's jobs was collecting rent from his father's tenants.

But Trump did not like collecting rent. He also did not like the physical labor involved in caring for residential **real estate**. He had bigger plans. He set his sights on Manhattan.

In 1971, Trump took control of the family business. He was 25 years old. He renamed the business the Trump Organization. He then moved from Queens to an apartment in Manhattan. There, he could spend more time with the city's influential people.

Trump's apartment was very different from his family's **plush** home in Queens. However, he did not spend much time there. Instead, he walked the streets of Manhattan deciding which buildings he wanted to own someday.

The Trump family home in Queens. Fred Trump built with red brick as it was a penny cheaper than tan brick.

THE BIG APPLE

Trump's goal was to develop **real estate** in Manhattan. He wanted his buildings to be fancy and gain lots of attention. He also wanted his projects to make a lot of money.

Trump's first major success was buying and **renovating** the Commodore Hotel. The 58-year-old hotel was run down. It was losing money every year. But it was next door to Grand Central Terminal. Trump thought the right hotel could prosper there.

Before he could begin, Trump had to get approval for the project. Real estate deals in New York involve many people and a lot of politics. Fred Trump helped his son get the approvals and financing needed to develop the property.

Trump completely renovated and modernized the hotel. It became the Grand Hyatt New York. It opened in 1980.

In the meantime, Trump had married fashion model Ivana Zelníčková in 1977. Ivana had **immigrated** from Czechoslovakia in the 1970s. She met Trump in New York City in 1976. The couple had three children, Donald Jr., Ivanka, and Eric.

(Left to right) *Donald Jr., Ivana, Ivanka, and Eric*

BUILDING ON SUCCESS

Trump continued to develop high-profile **real estate** projects. In 1983, he opened the 58-story Trump Tower on New York's Fifth Avenue. At the time, it was the tallest all-glass building in Manhattan. It featured an 80-foot waterfall inside a six-story atrium lined with pink marble.

In the 1980s, Trump began investing in gambling facilities in Atlantic City, New Jersey. His properties there eventually included Trump Plaza, Trump Castle, and Trump Taj Mahal.

Eventually, Trump expanded his business beyond real estate. In 1983, he bought the New Jersey Generals of the United States Football League. Five years later, he acquired the Eastern Air Lines Shuttle and renamed it the Trump Shuttle.

In 1987, Trump worked with a professional writer to write *The Art of the Deal*. In it, Trump explained how some of his most successful deals had been made. The book reached number one on the *New York Times* Best Sellers list.

Trump Taj Mahal was the largest hotel-casino in the world.

HARD TIMES

Trump was very successful. He was on *Forbes* magazine's World Billionaires list. But a **stock market** crash in 1987 led to a **recession** in the early 1990s. The country's **real estate** market declined. Suddenly, Trump's properties were worth less than they had been before. In addition, his casinos were not making enough money.

Trump also had a lot of **debt**. He found himself unable to repay the money he owed. His casino companies went into **bankruptcy**. He had to borrow more money and give up some of his properties to pay the debt.

Trump: The Game was originally released in 1989. It was released again after the success of The Apprentice.

At the same time, Trump's marriage to Ivana was nearing an end. The two divorced in 1991. Two years later, he married actress Marla Maples. They had a daughter, Tiffany. Trump and Maples divorced in 1999.

Marla Maples (left) *and Tiffany Trump*

THE COMEBACK

As the 1990s progressed, the **economy** improved. So did Trump's fortunes. In 1996, he joined with television network NBC to buy the Miss Universe Organization. This group produced the Miss America, Miss USA, and Miss Teen USA beauty pageants.

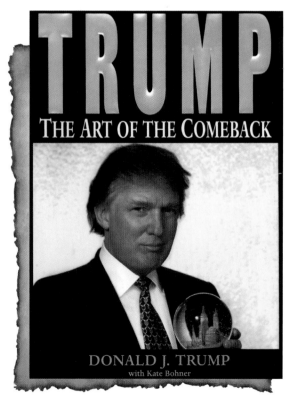

Trump continued to develop **real estate** projects. These would include New York's Trump World Tower, the Trump International Hotel and Tower in Chicago, Illinois, the Trump Hotel in Las Vegas, Nevada, and Trump World in Seoul, South Korea.

Trump cowrote another book, *The Art of the Comeback*, in 1997. It told how he had succeeded in business despite a weak economy.

The Art of the Comeback *was a* New York Times *best seller.*

20

Trump owns 17 golf courses around the world.

Trump began playing golf as a student at the University of Pennsylvania. In 1999, he opened the Trump International Golf Course in West Palm Beach, Florida. It was the first of many golf courses he would own around the world.

TELEVISION STAR

Trump was now back on more solid financial footing. Having succeeded in **real estate** and entertainment, he was ready for his next challenge.

In 2004, Trump began starring in a reality television show called *The Apprentice*. The program featured would-be employees competing in a number of challenges in order to secure a job with him. When they failed, Trump would tell them "You're fired!" The phrase quickly became part of popular **culture**.

The following year, Trump married model Melania Knauss. Knauss was born in Slovenia. The two had met at a party in 1998. Their son Barron was born in 2006.

Two years later, Trump began *The Celebrity Apprentice*. On this program, the contestants were well-known people in the world of news and entertainment.

Trump's television shows were very popular. He was nominated for an Emmy Award for Outstanding Reality-competition Program twice for *The Apprentice*. In 2007, he received a star on the Hollywood Walk of Fame.

Trump accepted his Hollywood Walk of Fame star with his wife Melania and his son Barron.

CANDIDATE TRUMP

In June 2015, Trump announced he was running for the **Republican** Party presidential nomination. Many people were **skeptical**. In 2000, Trump had run on the **Reform** Party ticket. And, he was once a member of the **Democratic** Party too.

During his campaign, Trump made comments that made many voters uneasy. He proposed building a wall along the country's border with Mexico to stop illegal **immigration**. He also proposed a ban on allowing **Muslims** to immigrate to the US.

Despite these and other remarks, Trump's popularity increased. His supporters believed his record as a business leader would make him a good president. Others liked him because he was not a Washington insider. They supported his positions on the **economy**, illegal immigration, and terrorism.

On July 18, 2016, Republicans gathered in Cleveland, Ohio, for the Republican National Convention. Party leaders such as Arizona senator John McCain and former president George W. Bush did not support Trump. They refused to attend. But on July 19, Trump clinched the Republican nomination. He chose Indiana governor Mike Pence as his **running mate**.

Before being elected Indiana's governor in 2012, Pence (right) was a six-term US congressman.

THE BIG DEAL

The **Democrats** had nominated Hillary Clinton as their candidate. Her **running mate** was Virginia governor Tim Kaine. Clinton was the first woman nominee from either the Democratic or **Republican** Parties.

Clinton was no stranger to the White House. She was First Lady from 1993 through 2001 when her husband, Bill Clinton, was president. She had served two terms as senator from New York and was **secretary of state** under President Barack Obama.

The campaign was full of hostility. Clinton accused Trump of behaving inappropriately toward women. Trump said Clinton was rigging the election. Republican Party officials withdrew their support of Trump's campaign. Clinton was widely favored to win.

But millions of Americans stood behind Trump. They believed in his message. And Clinton was facing an investigation. Officials were looking into her handling of secure information. This caused her popularity to fall. On November 8, 2016, voters went to the polls.

Clinton and Trump met for three debates before the election. The campaign was so combative that they only shook hands at the first one.

PRESIDENT TRUMP

Voter turnout was high all over the country. To win, a presidential candidate must get 270 **Electoral College** votes. As polls closed across the nation, results showed Trump had defeated Clinton. He was projected to win 306 Electoral College votes. Clinton was expected to receive 232.

On the way to victory, Trump had defeated 16 **Republican** candidates to win the party's presidential nomination. In Clinton, he had faced an experienced politician who had the full support of her party. But in spite of these challenges, Trump closed the biggest deal of his career.

In his acceptance speech, Trump vowed his **administration** would repair the nation's **infrastructure** and improve its **economy**. In light of the divisive campaign, he asked Americans to come together again. He pledged to be president of all Americans.

President Trump was 70 years old when he took office.
He was the oldest person to serve as president.

OFFICE OF THE PRESIDENT

BRANCHES OF GOVERNMENT

The US government is divided into three branches. They are the executive, legislative, and judicial branches. This division is called a separation of powers. Each branch has some power over the others. This is called a system of checks and balances.

EXECUTIVE BRANCH

The executive branch enforces laws. It is made up of the president, the vice president, and the president's cabinet. The president represents the United States around the world. He or she oversees relations with other countries and signs treaties. The president signs bills into law and appoints officials and federal judges. He or she also leads the military and manages government workers.

LEGISLATIVE BRANCH

The legislative branch makes laws, maintains the military, and regulates trade. It also has the power to declare war. This branch consists of the Senate and the House of Representatives. Together, these two houses make up Congress. Each state has two senators. A state's population determines the number of representatives it has.

JUDICIAL BRANCH

The judicial branch interprets laws. It consists of district courts, courts of appeals, and the Supreme Court. District courts try cases. If a person disagrees with a trial's outcome, he or she may appeal. If the courts of appeals support the ruling, a person may appeal to the Supreme Court. The Supreme Court also makes sure that laws follow the US Constitution.

QUALIFICATIONS FOR OFFICE

To be president, a person must meet three requirements. A candidate must be at least 35 years old and a natural-born US citizen. He or she must also have lived in the United States for at least 14 years.

ELECTORAL COLLEGE

The US presidential election is an indirect election. Voters from each state choose electors to represent them in the Electoral College. The number of electors from each state is based on population. Each elector has one electoral vote. Electors are pledged to cast their vote for the candidate who receives the highest number of popular votes in their state. A candidate must receive the majority of Electoral College votes to win.

TERM OF OFFICE

Each president may be elected to two four-year terms. Sometimes, a president may only be elected once. This happens if he or she served more than two years of the previous president's term.

The presidential election is held on the Tuesday after the first Monday in November. The president is sworn in on January 20 of the following year. At that time, he or she takes the oath of office:

I do solemnly swear (or affirm) that I will faithfully execute the office of President of the United States, and will to the best of my ability, preserve, protect and defend the Constitution of the United States.

LINE OF SUCCESSION

The Presidential Succession Act of 1947 defines who becomes president if the president cannot serve. The vice president is first in the line of succession. Next are the Speaker of the House and the President Pro Tempore of the Senate. If none of these individuals is able to serve, the office falls to the president's cabinet members. They would take office in the order in which each department was created:

Secretary of State

Secretary of the Treasury

Secretary of Defense

Attorney General

Secretary of the Interior

Secretary of Agriculture

Secretary of Commerce

Secretary of Labor

Secretary of Health and Human Services

Secretary of Housing and Urban Development

Secretary of Transportation

Secretary of Energy

Secretary of Education

Secretary of Veterans Affairs

Secretary of Homeland Security

Benefits

- While in office, the president receives a salary of $400,000 each year. He or she lives in the White House and has 24-hour Secret Service protection.

- The president may travel on a Boeing 747 jet called Air Force One. The airplane can accommodate 70 passengers. It has kitchens, a dining room, sleeping areas, and a conference room. It also has fully equipped offices with the latest communications systems. Air Force One can fly halfway around the world before needing to refuel. It can even refuel in flight!

- If the president wishes to travel by car, he or she uses Cadillac One. Cadillac One is a Cadillac Deville. It has been modified with heavy armor and communications systems. The president takes Cadillac One along when visiting other countries if secure transportation will be needed.

- The president also travels on a helicopter called Marine One. Like the presidential car, Marine One accompanies the president when traveling abroad if necessary.

- Sometimes, the president needs to get away and relax with family and friends. Camp David is the official presidential retreat. It is located in the cool, wooded mountains in Maryland. The US Navy maintains the retreat, and the US Marine Corps keeps it secure. The camp offers swimming, tennis, golf, and hiking.

- When the president leaves office, he or she receives lifetime Secret Service protection. He or she also receives a yearly pension of $203,700 and funding for office space, supplies, and staff.

PRESIDENTS AND THEIR TERMS

PRESIDENT	PARTY	TOOK OFFICE	LEFT OFFICE	TERMS SERVED	VICE PRESIDENT
George Washington	None	April 30, 1789	March 4, 1797	Two	John Adams
John Adams	Federalist	March 4, 1797	March 4, 1801	One	Thomas Jefferson
Thomas Jefferson	Democratic-Republican	March 4, 1801	March 4, 1809	Two	Aaron Burr, George Clinton
James Madison	Democratic-Republican	March 4, 1809	March 4, 1817	Two	George Clinton, Elbridge Gerry
James Monroe	Democratic-Republican	March 4, 1817	March 4, 1825	Two	Daniel D. Tompkins
John Quincy Adams	Democratic-Republican	March 4, 1825	March 4, 1829	One	John C. Calhoun
Andrew Jackson	Democrat	March 4, 1829	March 4, 1837	Two	John C. Calhoun, Martin Van Buren
Martin Van Buren	Democrat	March 4, 1837	March 4, 1841	One	Richard M. Johnson
William H. Harrison	Whig	March 4, 1841	April 4, 1841	Died During First Term	John Tyler
John Tyler	Whig	April 6, 1841	March 4, 1845	Completed Harrison's Term	Office Vacant
James K. Polk	Democrat	March 4, 1845	March 4, 1849	One	George M. Dallas
Zachary Taylor	Whig	March 5, 1849	July 9, 1850	Died During First Term	Millard Fillmore

PRESIDENT	PARTY	TOOK OFFICE	LEFT OFFICE	TERMS SERVED	VICE PRESIDENT
Millard Fillmore	Whig	July 10, 1850	March 4, 1853	Completed Taylor's Term	Office Vacant
Franklin Pierce	Democrat	March 4, 1853	March 4, 1857	One	William R.D. King
James Buchanan	Democrat	March 4, 1857	March 4, 1861	One	John C. Breckinridge
Abraham Lincoln	Republican	March 4, 1861	April 15, 1865	Served One Term, Died During Second Term	Hannibal Hamlin, Andrew Johnson
Andrew Johnson	Democrat	April 15, 1865	March 4, 1869	Completed Lincoln's Second Term	Office Vacant
Ulysses S. Grant	Republican	March 4, 1869	March 4, 1877	Two	Schuyler Colfax, Henry Wilson
Rutherford B. Hayes	Republican	March 3, 1877	March 4, 1881	One	William A. Wheeler
James A. Garfield	Republican	March 4, 1881	September 19, 1881	Died During First Term	Chester Arthur
Chester Arthur	Republican	September 20, 1881	March 4, 1885	Completed Garfield's Term	Office Vacant
Grover Cleveland	Democrat	March 4, 1885	March 4, 1889	One	Thomas A. Hendricks
Benjamin Harrison	Republican	March 4, 1889	March 4, 1893	One	Levi P. Morton
Grover Cleveland	Democrat	March 4, 1893	March 4, 1897	One	Adlai E. Stevenson
William McKinley	Republican	March 4, 1897	September 14, 1901	Served One Term, Died During Second Term	Garret A. Hobart, Theodore Roosevelt

PRESIDENTS 13–25, 1850–1901

PRESIDENT	PARTY	TOOK OFFICE	LEFT OFFICE	TERMS SERVED	VICE PRESIDENT
Theodore Roosevelt	Republican	September 14, 1901	March 4, 1909	Completed McKinley's Second Term, Served One Term	Office Vacant, Charles Fairbanks
William Taft	Republican	March 4, 1909	March 4, 1913	One	James S. Sherman
Woodrow Wilson	Democrat	March 4, 1913	March 4, 1921	Two	Thomas R. Marshall
Warren G. Harding	Republican	March 4, 1921	August 2, 1923	Died During First Term	Calvin Coolidge
Calvin Coolidge	Republican	August 3, 1923	March 4, 1929	Completed Harding's Term, Served One Term	Office Vacant, Charles Dawes
Herbert Hoover	Republican	March 4, 1929	March 4, 1933	One	Charles Curtis
Franklin D. Roosevelt	Democrat	March 4, 1933	April 12, 1945	Served Three Terms, Died During Fourth Term	John Nance Garner, Henry A. Wallace, Harry S. Truman
Harry S. Truman	Democrat	April 12, 1945	January 20, 1953	Completed Roosevelt's Fourth Term, Served One Term	Office Vacant, Alben Barkley
Dwight D. Eisenhower	Republican	January 20, 1953	January 20, 1961	Two	Richard Nixon
John F. Kennedy	Democrat	January 20, 1961	November 22, 1963	Died During First Term	Lyndon B. Johnson
Lyndon B. Johnson	Democrat	November 22, 1963	January 20, 1969	Completed Kennedy's Term, Served One Term	Office Vacant, Hubert H. Humphrey
Richard Nixon	Republican	January 20, 1969	August 9, 1974	Completed First Term, Resigned During Second Term	Spiro T. Agnew, Gerald Ford

PRESIDENTS 26–37, 1901–1974

PRESIDENT	PARTY	TOOK OFFICE	LEFT OFFICE	TERMS SERVED	VICE PRESIDENT
Gerald Ford	Republican	August 9, 1974	January 20, 1977	Completed Nixon's Second Term	Nelson A. Rockefeller
Jimmy Carter	Democrat	January 20, 1977	January 20, 1981	One	Walter Mondale
Ronald Reagan	Republican	January 20, 1981	January 20, 1989	Two	George H.W. Bush
George H.W. Bush	Republican	January 20, 1989	January 20, 1993	One	Dan Quayle
Bill Clinton	Democrat	January 20, 1993	January 20, 2001	Two	Al Gore
George W. Bush	Republican	January 20, 2001	January 20, 2009	Two	Dick Cheney
Barack Obama	Democrat	January 20, 2009	January 20, 2017	Two	Joe Biden
Donald Trump	Republican	January 20, 2017			Mike Pence

"We must reclaim our country's destiny and dream big and bold and daring." Donald Trump

WRITE TO THE PRESIDENT

You may write to the president at:

**The White House
1600 Pennsylvania Avenue NW
Washington, DC 20500**

You may e-mail the president at:
comments@whitehouse.gov

GLOSSARY

administration - a group of people that manages an operation, a department, or an office. An administrator is a person who works for an administration.

bankruptcy - the state of having been legally declared unable to pay a debt.

borough - one of five divisions of New York City. They are Manhattan, the Bronx, Queens, Brooklyn, and Staten Island.

culture - the customs, arts, and tools of a nation or people at a certain time.

debt (DEHT) - something owed to someone, especially money.

Democrat - a member of the Democratic political party. Democrats believe in social change and strong government.

discipline - training that molds, corrects, or perfects something.

economy - the way a nation uses its money, goods, and natural resources. Economics is the science of this. An economist is a person who is an expert in this.

Electoral College - the group of representatives that elects the US president and vice president by casting electoral votes. Each state has a certain number of representatives, or electors, based on population. Electors cast their votes for the candidate who received the most popular votes in their state.

immigrate - to enter another country to live. A person who immigrates is called an immigrant.

infrastructure - the basic framework of public society. It includes a community's government, transportation, and education systems.

Muslim - a person who follows Islam. Islam is a religion based on the teachings of the prophet Muhammad as they appear in the Koran.

negotiate (nih-GOH-shee-ayt) - to work out an agreement about the terms of a contract.

plush - very fancy and usually expensive.

real estate - property, including buildings and land. It is also the business of buying and selling such property.

recession - a period of time when business activity slows.

Reform - a political party founded in 1995. It seeks to reform national politics, balance the federal budget, repay the national debt, and reform the tax code.

renovate - to restore by rebuilding or repairing.

Republican - a member of the Republican political party. Republicans are conservative and believe in small government.

running mate - a candidate running for a lower-rank position on an election ticket, especially the candidate for vice president.

secretary of state - a member of the president's cabinet who heads the US Department of State. This department handles relations with other countries.

sibling - a brother or a sister.

skeptical - having or expressing doubt about something.

stock market - a place where stocks and bonds, which represent parts of businesses, are bought and sold.

thrift - careful use of money so that it is not wasted.

WEBSITES

To learn more about the United States Presidents, visit **booklinks.abdopublishing.com**. These links are routinely monitored and updated to provide the most current information available.

INDEX